Classic

BRITISH

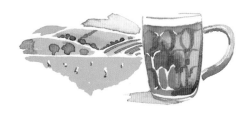

Classic
BRITISH

Authentic and delicious regional dishes

FOREWORD BY
SUE LAWRENCE

© 1996 Anness Publishing Limited

This edition published in 1996 by
SMITHMARK Publishers, a division of US Media Holdings, Inc
16 East 32nd Street
New York NY 10016
USA

SMITHMARK books are available for bulk purchase for sales promotion and for premium use. For details write or call
the Manager of Special Sales, SMITHMARK Publishers, 16 East 32nd Street, New York, NY 10016; (212) 532–6600.

Produced by Anness Publishing Limited
1 Boundary Row
London SE1 8HP

Publisher Joanna Lorenz
Senior Cookery Editor Linda Fraser
Cookery Editor Anne Hildyard
Designer Nigel Partridge
Illustrations Madeleine David
Photographers Karl Adamson, Steve Baxter, James Duncan and Michael Michaels
Recipes Alex Barker, Roz Denny, Christine France, Annie Nichols and Steven Wheeler
Food for photography Carole Handslip, Wendy Lee and Jane Stevenson
Stylists Madeleine Brehaut, Hilary Guy, Blake Minton and Kirsty Rawlings
Jacket photography Amanda Heywood

Typeset by MC Typeset Ltd, Rochester, Kent
Printed and bound in China

CONTENTS

FOREWORD

Traditional British food has enjoyed a comeback in recent years. Not that it ever went away in most homes throughout Britain, but it did fade into insignificance in many restaurant kitchens. Today, however, there is renewed pride in our time-honoured recipes, a realization that not only do we have possibly the best larder in the world, but also some of the finest dishes. Now both the home cook and the *chef de cuisine* are once again proudly presenting great British classics like Kedgeree, Roast Beef with Yorkshire Puddings, and Shepherd's Pie.

Regional dishes also feature in this collection: try, for instance, Scotch Broth, that rich rib-sticking soup which, along with porridge, has fortified Scots for generations, or Glamorgan Sausages, vegetarian treats made from leeks and Caerphilly cheese. The recipe for Irish Stew is a good example of how old-fashioned dishes can be updated: classically made with mutton, the recipe here is for middle neck lamb chops, which are readily available and far more tender.

Some recipes are inspired by the seasons. Scottish Salmon with Herb Butter, and Summer Pudding are synonymous with hot summer days, while Pheasant with Mushrooms, followed by Apple and Blackberry Nut Crumble would make a marvellous autumn menu. Lamb and Spring Vegetable Stew, and Rhubarb and Orange Fool are perfect for spring. As for winter, what could be more satisfying than Steak, Kidney and Mushroom Pie?

Another interesting feature of the book is the use of British farmhouse cheeses. Seeking sources for these, and other fine ingredients, can be a journey in itself, both literally and figuratively. Read the recipes, get to know your suppliers – local and further afield – and rediscover the considerable culinary pleasures of *Classic British* dishes.

SUE LAWRENCE

INTRODUCTION

Great British cooking is essentially fresh and simple, relying for its success on the flavour of some of the world's finest raw materials. Scotch beef, Welsh lamb, Colchester oysters, Devonshire clotted cream – many of the most sought-after ingredients evoke images of a rural Britain with a strong farming tradition, where small communities created regional specialities that survive and even flourish today.

Beef, lamb, pork and poultry have been reared here for hun-

dreds of years. The British perfected the art of roasting, as well as the long, slow cooking of stews and braised dishes. Pastries – not the delicate confections of the French but no-nonsense pastries, raised pies and suet puddings – are British specialities, as are cakes, biscuits and breads for every occasion.

Island communities inevitably develop a wide range of fish and shellfish recipes, and Britain is no exception. Fish and chips is regarded by many visitors as the British national dish, but frying is just one cooking method. Fish is grilled, poached, soused, stir-fried, steamed, smoked, baked and barbecued. Country

Three typical British scenes: harvesting wheat at the end of summer (left), that quintessential British activity; cricket, played on the rolling South Downs (above), fresh vegetables displayed to perfection at the Chelsea flower show (right).

sports – an integral part of British rural life – provide game such as pheasant, grouse and venison.

British dairies, from the large factories to the small farmhouse units, make a wide variety of produce, including cream, yogurt, butter and cheese. Cheesemaking is a proud tradition, with many regional specialities taking their names from the places where they were originally made. Cheddar is a typical example. A hard cheese, it has been produced in the Cheddar area in Somerset since the days of Henry II, and is today the most widely made cheese in the world. Stilton, often referred to as the king of English cheeses, originated three centuries ago, and was made popular by the Bell Inn in Stilton. Even now, it can only be made in certain counties: that of Derbyshire, Leicestershire and Nottinghamshire.

Fruit and vegetable crops have also led to traditions in the regions where they are grown. For example, from the orchards in the west country came the cider industry (see the recipe for Country Cider Hot-Pot on page 36) and the soft fruits of garden and hedgerow are used in several classic recipes, including the inimitable Summer Pudding and that autumn favourite, Apple and Blackberry Nut Crumble (see pages 54 and 56). Vegetables, particularly root vegetables, are staple foods, with Ireland justly famous for its potatoes, and Wales for its leeks.

Cereals crops, including wheat, barley and oats, are responsible for such diverse dishes as porridge, scones, crumpets, cakes, biscuits and breads. Afternoon tea, that great British ritual, is a tribute to the baker's art.

As its title suggests, this collection of recipes includes many classic British favourites, from Potted Prawns and Scotch Broth to Old English Trifle and Summer Berry Medley, dishes as relevant to today's lifestyle as ever they were, just waiting to be rediscovered and enjoyed.

SCOTTISH SALMON WITH HERB BUTTER

This is a delightfully simple way to serve salmon steaks. The dill, with lemon rind and juice, give a lovely piquancy to the butter but they do not overpower the delicate flavour of the fish.

INGREDIENTS
50g/2 oz/4 tbsp butter, softened
finely grated rind of ½ lemon
15ml/1 tbsp lemon juice
15ml/1 tbsp chopped fresh dill
butter, for greasing
4 salmon steaks
2 lemon slices, halved
4 fresh dill sprigs
salt and ground black pepper
new potatoes and green salad, to sern

SERVES 4

COOK'S TIP
You can use other fresh herbs to flavour the butter – try mint, fennel fronds, lemon balm, parsley or oregano instead of the dill.

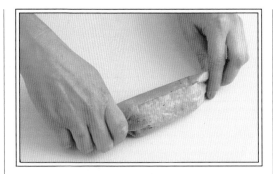

1 Place the butter, lemon rind and juice, chopped dill and seasoning in a small bowl and mix together with a fork until blended. Spoon the herb butter on to a piece of greaseproof paper and roll up, smoothing into a sausage shape. Twist the ends tightly, wrap in clear film and put in the freezer for 20 minutes until firm.

2 Meanwhile, preheat the oven to 190°C/375°F/Gas 5. Cut out four squares of foil big enough to encase the salmon steaks and grease lightly. Place a salmon steak in the centre of each one.

3 Remove the herb butter roll from the freezer. Leave to stand for a few minutes. Using a sharp knife, slice the butter into eight rounds. Place two rounds on top of each salmon steak, with a halved lemon slice in the centre and a sprig of dill on top.

4 Lift up the edges of the foil and crinkle them together to seal. Place the parcels on a baking sheet and bake for about 20 minutes. Remove from the oven, open the parcels and slide the contents on to warmed plates with the juices. Serve hot, with new potatoes and a fresh, crisp green salad.

BROCCOLI AND STILTON SOUP

A really easy, but rich, soup which is perfect served as a light lunch or supper, accompanied by crusty bread, cheese and salad.

INGREDIENTS
350g/12oz broccoli
25g/1oz/2 tbsp butter
1 onion, chopped
1 leek, white part only, chopped
1 small potato, cut into chunks
600ml/1 pint/2½ cups hot chicken stock
300ml/½ pint/1¼ cups milk
45ml/3 tbsp double cream
115g/4oz Stilton cheese, rind removed, crumbled
salt and ground black pepper

SERVES 4

1 Break the broccoli into florets, discarding any tough stems. Set aside two small florets for the garnish.

2 Melt the butter in a large saucepan and cook the onion and leek until soft but not coloured. Add the broccoli and potato, then pour in the stock. Cover the pan and simmer for 15–20 minutes, until the vegetables are tender.

3 Cool slightly, then purée. Strain through a sieve back into the pan. Add the milk, cream and seasoning, and reheat gently. Finally, add the cheese, stirring until it just melts. Do not boil.

4 Meanwhile, blanch the reserved florets and slice vertically (*left*). Serve the soup in warmed bowls, garnished with the florets and a grinding of black pepper.

SCOTCH BROTH

S ustaining and warming, Scotch Broth is custom-made for chilly Scottish weather, and makes a delicious winter soup anywhere.

INGREDIENTS

1kg/2¼lb lean neck of lamb, cubed
1.75 litres/3 pints/7½ cups water
1 large onion, chopped
50g/2oz/¼ cup pearl barley
bouquet garni or a few sprigs of parsley and a bay leaf
1 large carrot, chopped
1 turnip, chopped
3 leeks, chopped
½ small white cabbage, shredded
salt and ground black pepper

SERVES 6–8

1 Put the lamb and water into a large saucepan and bring to the boil. Skim off any grey foam, then stir in the onion, pearl barley and bouquet garni or herbs.

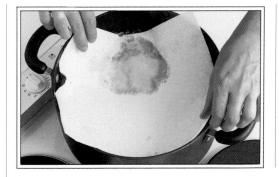

2 Bring the soup back to the boil, then partly cover the pan and simmer gently for 1 hour. Add the remaining vegetables and the seasoning. Bring to the boil again, partly cover and simmer for 35 minutes.

3 Use kitchen paper to remove surplus fat from the top of the soup (*left*). Discard the bouquet garni or herbs and serve hot.

GLAMORGAN SAUSAGES

These tasty sausages are ideal for vegetarians as they are made from cheese and leeks rather than meat. They are delicious for a leisurely breakfast.

INGREDIENTS
150g/5oz/2½ cups fresh breadcrumbs
150g/5oz/generous 1 cup grated
Caerphilly cheese
1 small leek, very finely chopped
15ml/1 tbsp chopped fresh parsley
1.5ml/¼ tsp chopped fresh thyme
2 eggs
7.5ml/1½ tsp English mustard powder
about 45ml/3 tbsp milk
plain flour, for coating
15ml/1 tbsp oil
15g/½oz/1 tbsp butter, melted
salt and ground black pepper
mixed salad, to serve

MAKES 8

COOK'S TIP
If you prefer a really strong cheese flavour, use mature Cheddar cheese instead of Caerphilly. For a truly authentic touch, but not for vegetarians, fry the sausages in bacon fat.

1 Mix the breadcrumbs, cheese, leek, parsley, thyme and seasoning. Whisk the eggs with the mustard and reserve 30ml/2 tbsp. Stir remaining egg mixture into the cheese mixture, adding enough milk to bind.

2 Turn out the cheese mixture on to a lightly floured surface and divide into eight equal pieces. Using your hands, form the mixture into eight sausages.

3 Dip the sausages into the reserved egg mixture to coat. Season the flour with salt and pepper, then roll the sausages in the seasoned flour to give a light, even coating. Chill for about 30 minutes until firm.

4 Preheat the grill and oil the grill rack. Mix together the oil and melted butter and brush over the sausages. Grill the sausages for 5–10 minutes, turning occasionally, until golden brown all over. Serve hot or cold with a mixed salad.

FISH CAKES

For extra-special fish cakes, you could use canned salmon, drained, or even fresh cooked salmon. The better the quality and flavour of the fish, the nicer the fish cakes will be.

INGREDIENTS
450g/1lb potatoes, cooked and mashed
450g/1lb mixed white and smoked fish,
such as haddock or cod, cooked and flaked
25g/1oz/2 tbsp butter, cubed
45ml/3 tbsp chopped fresh parsley
1 egg, separated
flour, for shaping
1 egg, beaten
about 50g/2oz/1 cup fine breadcrumbs,
made with day-old bread
vegetable oil, for frying
ground black pepper
mixed salad, to serve (optional)

SERVES 4

1 Place the potatoes in a bowl and beat in the flaked fish, butter, parsley and egg yolk. Season with pepper.

2 Turn out the fish mixture on to a lightly floured surface and divide into eight equal portions. With floured hands, form each one into a flat cake.

3 Tip the egg white into a bowl, add the whole egg and beat until frothy. Scatter the breadcrumbs on to a plate. Dip each fish cake first into the beaten egg mixture, then into the breadcrumbs.

4 Heat the oil in a frying pan, then fry the fish cakes in batches for about 3–5 minutes on each side, until crisp and golden. Drain on kitchen paper and serve hot with a mixed salad if wished.

COOK'S TIP
To add extra piquancy to fish cakes, stir a little Worcestershire sauce or anchovy essence into the fish mixture and add a pinch of cayenne pepper or grated nutmeg.

POTTED PRAWNS

The tiny brown shrimps traditionally used for potting in butter are very time-consuming to peel. Since they are hard to find nowadays, it is easier to use peeled, cooked prawns instead.

INGREDIENTS
225g/8oz peeled, cooked prawns
225g/8oz/1 cup butter
pinch of ground mace
pinch of cayenne pepper
salt
fresh dill sprigs, to garnish
lemon wedges and thin slices of brown bread and butter, to serve

SERVES 4

1 Chop a quarter of the prawns. Melt half of the butter slowly, carefully skimming off any foam that rises to the surface. Stir all the prawns, the mace, salt and cayenne pepper into the pan and heat gently without boiling. Spoon the prawn and butter mixture into four individual pots or ramekins (*left*) · and leave to cool.

2 Heat the remaining butter in a clean small saucepan, then carefully spoon the clear butter over the prawn mixture, leaving behind the sediment.

3 Leave the prawn mixture until the butter is almost set, then place a dill sprig in the centre of each pot or ramekin. Leave to set completely, then cover and chill.

4 Remove from the fridge 30 minutes before serving with lemon wedges and thin slices of brown bread and butter.

KEDGEREE

Popular for breakfast and supper in the nineteenth century, Kedgeree has its origins in *khichri,* an Indian rice and lentil dish, and is often flavoured with curry powder.

INGREDIENTS
500g/1¼lb smoked haddock
115g/4oz/generous ½ cup long grain rice
butter, for greasing
30ml/2 tbsp lemon juice
150ml/¼ pint/⅔ cup single or
soured cream
pinch of freshly grated nutmeg
pinch of cayenne pepper
2 eggs, hard-boiled, peeled and cut
into wedges
50g/2oz/4 tbsp butter, cubed
30ml/2 tbsp chopped fresh parsley
salt and ground black pepper
fresh parsley sprigs, to garnish

SERVES 4

1 Poach the haddock, in water just to cover, for about 10 minutes, until the flesh flakes easily. Lift the fish from the cooking liquid using a slotted spoon, then remove any skin and bones and flake the flesh.

2 Pour the rice into a measuring jug and note the volume, then tip it out, pour the fish cooking liquid into the jug and top up with water, until it measures twice the volume of the rice.

3 Bring the fish cooking liquid to the boil, add the rice, stir, then cover and simmer for about 15 minutes, until the rice is tender and the liquid absorbed. While the rice is cooking, butter a baking dish and preheat the oven to 180°C/350°F/Gas 4.

4 Remove the rice from the heat and stir in the lemon juice, cream, flaked fish, nutmeg and cayenne pepper. Add the egg wedges to the rice mixture and stir in gently so they do not break up.

5 Tip the rice mixture into the baking dish, dot with butter, cover and bake for about 25 minutes. Stir in the chopped parsley, check the seasoning (smoked haddock is a salty fish so salt may not be necessary) and serve garnished with parsley sprigs.

ENGLISH PLOUGHMAN'S PATE

This cheese pâté provides a slight twist to the ploughman's lunch of bread, cheese and pickled onions. It is a modern version of the traditional English potted cheese and is delicious served with Melba toast.

INGREDIENTS
45ml/3 tbsp full-fat cream cheese
75g/3oz/¾ cup grated mild
Cheddar cheese
75g/3oz/¾ cup grated Double
Gloucester cheese
4 pickled onions, drained and
finely chopped
15ml/1 tbsp apricot chutney
25g/1oz/2 tbsp butter, melted
30ml/2 tbsp snipped fresh chives
salt and ground black pepper
4 slices soft grain bread
watercress and cherry tomatoes, to serve

SERVES 4

1 Mix together the cheeses, onions, chutney and butter in a bowl and season lightly. Spoon the mixture on to a sheet of greaseproof paper and roll up into a cylinder, smoothing the mixture into a roll with your hands. Scrunch the ends of the paper together and twist to seal. Put in the freezer for about 30 minutes, until just firm.

2 Spread the chives on to a plate, then unwrap the chilled cheese pâté. Roll in the chives until evenly coated. Wrap in clear film and chill for 10 minutes.

3 Preheat the grill. To make the Melba toast, toast the bread lightly on both sides. Cut off the crusts and slice each piece in half horizontally. Cut each half into four triangles. Grill, untoasted side up, until golden and curled at the edges.

4 Slice the pâté into rounds and serve three or four rounds per person with the toast, watercress and cherry tomatoes.

COOK'S TIP
To make potted cheese, grate 175g/6oz strong hard cheese and mix to a paste with 60g/2oz/4 tbsp butter, 2.5ml/½ tsp each English mustard powder and ground mace, 30ml/2 tbsp sweet sherry or to taste and a pinch of cayenne pepper. Pack into small pots and cover with a layer of melted butter.

SMOKED TROUT WITH CUCUMBER SALAD

Smoked trout provides an easy and delicious first course or light lunch. Serve it at room temperature for the best flavour.

INGREDIENTS
1 large cucumber
60ml/4 tbsp crème fraîche or Greek-style yogurt
15ml/1 tbsp chopped fresh dill
4 smoked trout fillets
salt and ground black pepper
fresh dill sprigs, to garnish
crusty wholemeal bread, to serve (optional)

SERVES 4

1 Peel the cucumber, halve it lengthways with a sharp knife and scoop out the seeds using a teaspoon. Cut the flesh into tiny dice.

2 Put the cucumber in a colander set over a plate and sprinkle with salt. Cover with a plate and weight down with kitchen weights or a can of food. Leave to drain for at least 1 hour to draw out the excess moisture.

3 Rinse the cucumber well, then pat dry on kitchen paper. Transfer to a bowl and stir in the crème fraîche or yogurt, chopped dill and some pepper (*left*). Chill the salad for about 30 minutes.

4 Arrange the trout fillets on individual plates with the salad and grind over a little black pepper. Garnish with dill sprigs and serve with wholemeal bread, if wished.

DEEP-FRIED SPICY SMELTS

A delicious dish of tiny crisp fish, best served very hot. If smelts are not available, whitebait, the small fry of sprats and herring, can be used instead.

INGREDIENTS
450g/1lb smelts
40g/1½oz/⅓ cup plain flour
5ml/1 tsp paprika
pinch of cayenne pepper
vegetable oil, for deep-frying
12 fresh parsley sprigs
salt and ground black pepper
8 lemon wedges, to garnish

SERVES 4

1 If using frozen smelts, defrost in the bag and pour away any water. Spread the fish out on kitchen paper and pat dry. Place the flour, paprika, cayenne pepper and the seasoning in a large plastic bag. Add the smelts and shake gently until all the fish are lightly coated with the flour, then transfer the floured smelts to a plate.

2 Heat about 5cm/2in of oil in a saucepan or deep-fat fryer to 190°C/375°F, or until a cube of bread dropped into the fat browns in 30 seconds.

3 Add the smelts in batches and deep-fry for 2–3 minutes, until lightly golden and crisp (*left*). Remove, drain on kitchen paper and keep warm while frying the rest.

4 Drop the parsley sprigs into the hot oil (don't worry if the oil spits a bit) and fry for a few seconds until crisp. Drain on kitchen paper. Serve the smelts with the parsley and lemon wedges.

ROAST BEEF WITH YORKSHIRE PUDDINGS

For this classic Sunday lunchtime meal, traditionally served with mustard and horseradish sauce, choose a joint of beef such as sirloin or rib, either on the bone or boned and rolled.

INGREDIENTS
1.75kg/4–4½lb joint of beef
30–60ml/2–4 tbsp beef dripping or oil
300ml/½ pint/1¼ cups vegetable or veal stock, wine or water
salt and ground black pepper
watercress sprigs, to garnish (optiona

FOR THE YORKSHIRE PUDDINGS
50g/2oz/½ cup plain flour
1 egg, beaten
150ml/¼ pint/⅔ cup milk
beef dripping or oil, for cooking

SERVES 6

1 Weigh the beef and calculate the cooking time. Allow 15 minutes per 450g/1lb plus 15 minutes for rare meat, 20 minutes plus 20 minutes for medium and 25–30 minutes plus 25 minutes for well-done.

2 Preheat the oven to 220°C/425°F/Gas 7. Heat the beef dripping or oil in a roasting tin in the oven.

3 Place the joint of beef on a rack, fat-side uppermost, then place the rack in the roasting tin.

4 Brush the beef with the dripping or oil, and cook for 10 minutes, then lower heat to 175°C/350°F/Gas 4.

5 To make the Yorkshire puddings, sift the flour, salt and pepper into a bowl and form a well. Pour in the egg, then slowly add the milk mixture, stirring to make a smooth batter. Leave to stand for 30 minutes.

6 A few minutes before the meat is ready, raise the temperature to 200°C/400°F/Gas 6. Spoon dripping or oil into each of 12 patty tins. Place in the oven. Remove the meat, season, cover loosely and keep warm.

7 When the oil is hot, quickly divide the batter among the patty tins. Bake for 15–20 minutes, until well risen and brown.

8 To make the gravy, spoon the fat from the roasting tin, leaving the meat juices in the tin. Add the stock, wine or  water, stirring to dislodge the sediment, and boil for a few minutes. Check the seasoning, then strain the gravy and pour into a warmed sauceboat and serve with the beef and Yorkshire puddings. Garnish with watercress, if using.

PHEASANT WITH MUSHROOMS

This is an ideal recipe for an older cock bird because the long cooking time tenderizes the meat. Pheasant has a good ratio of meat to carcass.

INGREDIENTS
1 pheasant, jointed
250ml/8fl oz/1 cup red wine
45ml/3 tbsp vegetable oil
60ml/4 tbsp sherry vinegar
1 large onion, chopped
2 rashers smoked bacon, cut into strips
350g/12oz chestnut mushrooms, sliced
3 anchovy fillets, soaked for 10 minutes and drained
350ml/12fl oz/1½ cups game, veal or chicken stock
bouquet garni
salt and ground black pepper

SERVES 2

1 Place the pheasant pieces in a dish, add the wine, half of the oil and half of the vinegar, and scatter over half of the onion. Season, then cover and leave to marinate in a cool place for 8–12 hours, turning the pheasant occasionally.

2 Preheat the oven to 160°C/325°F/Gas 3. Lift the pheasant from the marinade, reserving the marinade, and pat dry on kitchen paper. Heat the remaining oil in a flameproof casserole, then brown the pheasant joints. Transfer to a plate.

3 Add the bacon and the remaining onion to the casserole and cook until the onion is soft. Stir in the mushrooms and cook for about 3 minutes.

4 Stir in the anchovies and the remaining vinegar and boil until reduced. Add the reserved marinade, cook for 2 minutes, then add the stock and bouquet garni. Return the pheasant pieces to the casserole, cover and bake for about 1½ hours.

5 Transfer the pheasant to a warmed serving dish. Boil the cooking juices to reduce, then discard the bouquet garni. Pour the juices over the pheasant and serve.

SHEPHERD'S PIE

A great family favourite, this dish can be prepared ahead and baked when you are ready to serve it. When it is made with beef, it becomes a cottage pie.

INGREDIENTS

30ml/2 tbsp vegetable oil
1 onion, finely chopped
1 carrot, finely chopped
115g/4oz mushrooms, chopped
500g/1¼lb lean minced lamb
300ml/½ pint/1¼ cups brown veal stock
15ml/1 tbsp plain flour
1 bay leaf
10–15ml/2–3 tsp Worcestershire sauce
15ml/1 tbsp tomato purée
675g/1½lb potatoes, boiled
25g/1oz/2 tbsp butter
45ml/3 tbsp hot milk
15ml/1 tbsp chopped fresh tarragon, plus
a sprig to garnish
salt and ground black pepper

SERVES 4

1 Heat the oil in a saucepan, add the onion, carrot and mushrooms and cook, stirring occasionally, until browned. Stir the lamb into the pan and cook, stirring to break up the lumps, until lightly browned.

2 Blend a few spoonfuls of the stock with the flour, then stir this mixture into the pan. Pour in the remaining stock and bring to a simmer, stirring constantly. Add the bay leaf, Worcestershire sauce and tomato purée, then cover the pan and cook very gently for 1 hour, stirring occasionally. Remove the lid from the pan towards the end of cooking to allow any excess water to evaporate, if necessary, but do not let it boil dry or stick to the pan.

3 Preheat the oven to 190°C/375°F/Gas 5. Heat the potatoes for 2 minutes, then mash with the butter, milk and seasoning.

4 Add the tarragon and seasoning to the mince mixture, then spoon into an ovenproof dish. Cover with an even layer of potato and make a pattern on the top with the prongs of a fork. Bake for 25 minutes, until golden brown. Serve hot, garnished with a sprig of tarragon.

LAMB AND SPRING VEGETABLE STEW

You could add a few blanched asparagus spears or young French beans to this cream-coloured stew when they are in season.

INGREDIENTS

65g/2½oz/5 tbsp butter
1kg/2¼lb lean boneless shoulder of lamb,
cut into 4cm/1½in cubes
600ml/1 pint/2½ cups lamb stock or water
150ml/¼ pint/⅔ cup dry white wine
1 onion, quartered
2 thyme sprigs
1 bay leaf
225g/8oz baby onions, halved
225g/8oz small young carrots
2 small turnips, quartered
175g/6oz shelled broad beans
15ml/1 tbsp plain flour
1 egg yolk
45ml/3 tbsp double cream
10ml/2 tsp lemon juice
salt and ground black pepper
30ml/2 tbsp chopped fresh
parsley, to garnish

SERVES 4

1 Melt 25g/1oz/2 tbsp of the butter in a large pan, add the lamb and sauté for about 2 minutes to seal the meat; do not allow it to colour. Pour in the stock or water and wine, bring to the boil, then skim the surface. Add the quartered onion, thyme and bay leaf. Cover and simmer for 1 hour.

2 Meanwhile, melt 15g/½oz/1 tbsp of the remaining butter in a frying pan over a moderate heat, add the baby onions and brown lightly.

3 Add the carrots, turnips and browned baby onions to the lamb and continue to cook for 20 minutes. Add the shelled broad beans and cook for a further 10 minutes, until the vegetables and lamb are tender.

4 Lift out the lamb and vegetables from the pan and arrange in a warmed serving dish. Cover and keep warm in a low oven.

5 Discard the onion quarters, thyme sprigs and bay leaf. Strain the stock and carefully skim off all the fat. Return the stock to the pan and boil rapidly over a high heat until the liquid has reduced to about 450ml/¾ pint/1⅞ cups.

6 Mix together the remaining butter and the flour to form a smooth paste. Whisk into the hot stock until thickened. Simmer for 2–3 minutes.

7 Blend together the egg yolk and cream in a bowl. Stir in a little of the hot stock mixture, then stir the egg yolk and cream mixture into the sauce. Reheat gently but do not boil. Add the lemon juice and season to taste with salt and pepper.

8 Pour the sauce over the lamb and vegetables, then sprinkle with the chopped parsley. Serve at once.

OATMEAL AND HERB RACK OF LAMB

Ask the butcher to remove the chine bone for you (this is the long bone that runs along the eye of the meat) – this will make carving easier.

INGREDIENTS
2 best end necks of lamb, about
1kg/2¼lb each
finely grated rind of 1 lemon
60ml/4 tbsp medium oatmeal
50g/2oz/1 cup fresh white breadcrumbs
60ml/4 tbsp chopped fresh parsley
25g/1oz/2 tbsp butter, melted
30ml/2 tbsp clear honey
salt and ground black pepper
fresh herb sprigs, to garnish
roasted baby vegetables and gravy, to
serve (optional)

SERVES 6

1 Preheat the oven to 200°C/400°F/Gas 6. Using a small sharp knife, cut through the skin and meat about 2.5cm/1in from the tips of the bones. Pull off the fatty meat to expose the bones, then scrape around each bone tip until completely clean.

2 Trim all the skin and most of the fat off the meat, then lightly score the fat. Repeat with the second rack.

3 Mix together the lemon rind, oatmeal, breadcrumbs, parsley and seasoning, then stir in the melted butter.

4 Brush the fatty side of each rack with honey, then press the oatmeal mixture evenly over the surface.

5 Place the racks in a roasting tin with the oatmeal uppermost. Roast for about 40–50 minutes, until cooked to taste. Cover loosely with foil if browning too much. To serve, slice each rack into three and garnish with herbs. Accompany with roasted baby vegetables and gravy made with the pan juices if wished.

IRISH STEW

Originally, Irish Stew was simply made with mutton, potatoes and onions. Mutton, which is now difficult to obtain, has a much fuller flavour than lamb so other ingredients have been added to the modern recipe to compensate.

INGREDIENTS

4 rashers smoked streaky bacon rashers, chopped
2 celery sticks, chopped
2 large onions, sliced
8 middle neck lamb chops, about 1kg/2¼lb total weight
1kg/2¼lb potatoes, sliced
300ml/½ pint/1¼ cups brown veal stock or water
5ml/1 tsp anchovy sauce
25ml/1½ tbsp Worcestershire sauce
salt and ground black pepper
chopped fresh parsley, to garnish

SERVES 4

1 Preheat the oven to 160°C/325°F/Gas 3. Fry the bacon for 3–5 minutes until the fat runs, then add the celery and a third of the onions and cook, stirring occasionally, until evenly browned.

2 Layer the chops, potatoes, bacon mixture and remaining onions in a casserole and season. Finish with potatoes.

3 Stir the veal stock or water, anchovy sauce and Worcestershire sauce into the bacon and vegetable cooking juices in the pan and bring to the boil. Pour the mixture into the casserole, adding some water if necessary so that the liquid comes halfway up the casserole.

4 Cover the casserole tightly, then cook in the oven for 3 hours, until the meat and vegetables are tender. Serve hot, sprinkled with parsley.

CHICKEN, LEEK AND PARSLEY PIE

The delicate flavours of chicken and leek complement each other well in this rich and filling pie. It makes a splendid meal for a winter's day.

INGREDIENTS

275g/10oz/2½ cups plain flour
pinch of salt
250g/9oz/generous 1 cup butter
2 egg yolks, plus a little beaten egg to glaze
3 part-boned chicken breasts
bouquet garni
8 black peppercorns
1 onion, quartered
1 carrot, roughly chopped
2 leeks, thinly sliced
50g/2oz Cheddar cheese, grated
25g/1oz Parmesan cheese, finely grated
45ml/3 tbsp chopped fresh parsley
30ml/2 tbsp wholegrain mustard
5ml/1 tsp cornflour
300ml/½ pint/1¼ cups double cream
salt and ground black pepper
mixed green salad, to serve (optional)

SERVES 4–6

1 To make the pastry, first sift the flour and salt. Blend together 200g/7oz/¾ cup butter and the egg yolks in a food processor or blender until creamy. Add the flour and process until the mixture is just coming together. Add 15ml/1 tbsp cold water and process for a few seconds. Turn out on to a lightly floured surface and knead lightly. Wrap in clear film and chill for about 1 hour.

2 Meanwhile, poach the chicken breasts in water to cover, with the bouquet garni, black peppercorns, onion and carrot until tender. Leave to cool in the liquid.

3 Preheat the oven to 200°C/400°F/Gas 6. Divide the pastry into two pieces, one slightly larger than the other. Roll out the larger piece on a lightly floured surface and use to line an 18 × 28cm/7 × 11in baking dish or tin. Prick the base with a fork and bake for 15 minutes. Leave to cool.

4 Lift the cooled chicken from the poaching liquid and discard the skin and bones. Cut the flesh into strips and set aside.

5 Melt the remaining butter in a frying pan and fry the leeks over a low heat, stirring occasionally, until soft. Stir in the cheeses and parsley. Spread half the leek mixture over the cooked pastry base, leaving a border all round. Cover the leek mixture with the chicken strips, then top with the remaining leek mixture.

6 Mix together the mustard, cornflour and cream in a small bowl. Add seasoning to taste, then pour over the filling.

7 Moisten the edges of the pastry base. Roll out the remaining pastry and cover the pie. Brush with beaten egg and bake for 30–40 minutes until golden and crisp. Serve hot, with a mixed green salad, if wished.

LAMB WITH MINT SAUCE

M int sauce, the traditional English accompaniment to lamb, may be made sweeter with more sugar or sharper with extra vinegar.

INGREDIENTS
8 lamb noisettes, 2–2.5cm/¾–1in thick
30ml/2 tbsp vegetable oil
45ml/3 tbsp dry white wine, or vegetable or veal stock
small sprigs of mint, to garnish
roasted new potatoes and carrots, to serve

FOR THE MINT SAUCE
30ml/2 tbsp boiling water
5–10ml/1–2 tsp sugar
bunch of fresh mint, finely chopped
about 30ml/2 tbsp white wine vinegar
salt and ground black pepper

SERVES 4

1 To make the mint sauce, stir the water and sugar together, then add the finely chopped mint, vinegar to taste and seasoning. Leave to stand for 30 minutes, to allow the flavours to mingle.

2 Season the lamb with pepper. Heat the oil in a large frying pan, then fry the lamb, in batches if necessary, for about 3 minutes on each side for pink meat.

3 Transfer the lamb to a warmed serving platter and season with salt, then cover and keep warm. Transfer the mint sauce to a jug or sauceboat.

4 Pour the wine or stock into the cooking juices and stir with a wooden spoon to dislodge the sediment from the bottom of the pan. Bring to the boil and let the juices bubble for a couple of minutes, then pour over the lamb. Serve the lamb noisettes at once with the mint sauce, potatoes and carrots, garnished with sprigs of mint.

BEEF IN GUINNESS

E ven if Guinness is not your chosen drink, try this recipe – you will be pleasantly surprised. It adds a delicious richness to the sauce.

INGREDIENTS

1kg/2¼lb chuck steak, cut into
4cm/1½in cubes
a little plain flour, for coating
45ml/3 tbsp vegetable oil
1 large onion, sliced
1 carrot, thinly sliced
2 celery sticks, thinly sliced
10ml/2 tsp sugar
5ml/1 tsp English mustard powder
15ml/1 tbsp tomato purée
2.5 × 7.5cm/1 × 3in strip orange rind
600ml/1 pint/2½ cups Guinness or other
dark stout
bouquet garni
salt and ground black pepper
fresh flat leaf parsley sprigs, to garnish

SERVES 6

1 Toss the beef in the flour to coat. Heat 30ml/2 tbsp of the oil in a large, shallow pan, then cook the beef in batches until lightly browned. Transfer to a bowl.

2 Add the remaining oil to the pan, then cook the onion until well browned, stirring occasionally and adding the carrot and celery towards the end.

3 Stir in the sugar, mustard, tomato purée, orange rind, Guinness and seasoning, then add the bouquet garni and bring to the boil. Return the meat, and any juices in the bowl, to the pan; add water, if necessary, so the meat is covered. Cover the pan tightly and cook gently for 2–2½ hours, until the meat is very tender. Serve, garnished with fresh flat leaf parsley sprigs.

COUNTRY CIDER HOT-POT

Game casseroles are a popular and healthy choice – and they are full of flavour too. If you cannot find wild rabbit, domestic rabbit pieces are available in supermarkets.

INGREDIENTS
30ml/2 tbsp flour
4 boneless rabbit pieces
25g/1oz/2 tbsp butter
15ml/1 tbsp vegetable oil
15 baby onions
4 lean bacon rashers, chopped
10ml/2 tsp Dijon mustard
450ml/¾ pint/1⅞ cups cider
3 carrots, chopped
2 parsnips, chopped
12 ready-to-eat prunes, stoned
1 fresh rosemary sprig
1 bay leaf
salt and ground black pepper
mashed potatoes, to serve (optional)

SERVES 4

1 Preheat the oven to 160°C/325°F/Gas 3. Place the flour and seasoning in a plastic bag, add the rabbit pieces and shake until coated. Remove from the bag and set aside.

2 Heat the butter and oil in a flameproof casserole and add the onions and bacon. Fry for 4 minutes until the onions have softened. Remove the onions and bacon with a slotted spoon and reserve.

3 Fry the seasoned rabbit pieces in the oil in the flameproof casserole until they are browned all over, then spread a little of the mustard over the top of each piece.

4 Return the onions and bacon to the pan. Pour on the cider and add the carrots, parsnips, prunes, rosemary and bay leaf. Season well. Bring to the boil, then cover and transfer to the oven. Cook for about 1½ hours, until tender.

5 Remove the rosemary sprig and bay leaf and serve the rabbit hot with creamy mashed potatoes if wished.

VARIATION
Rabbit is just as delicious cooked in beer as in cider. Omit the mustard, parsnips and rosemary and use pale ale instead of the cider and add 5ml/1 tsp crushed juniper berries with the chopped carrots and prunes.

BEEF WELLINGTON

B eef Wellington is supposedly so-named because of the resemblance of its shape and rich brown colour to the legs of the Duke of Wellington's boots.

INGREDIENTS
1.5kg/3½lb fillet of beef
30ml/2 tbsp vegetable oil
½ small onion, finely chopped
175g/6oz mushrooms, chopped
175g/6oz liver pâté
few drops each of lemon juice and
Worcestershire sauce
400g/14oz ready-made puff pastry
salt and ground black pepper
beaten egg, to glaze
fresh thyme sprigs, to garnish
green beans, to serve

1 Preheat the oven to 220°C/425°F/Gas 7. Season the beef, then tie it at intervals with string. Heat the oil in a roasting tin. Brown the beef over a high heat, then cook in the oven for 20 minutes. Leave to cool, then remove the string.

2 Scrape the cooking juices into a pan, add the onion and mushrooms and cook until tender. Cool, then mix with the pâté. Add the lemon juice and Worcestershire sauce.

3 Roll out the pastry to a large rectangle 5mm/¼in thick. Spread the pâté mixture over the beef, then place the beef on the pastry. Damp the edges and fold over to make a parcel (*left*). Press to seal.

4 Place on a baking sheet with the join underneath and brush with the egg. Bake for 20–45 minutes, until done to your liking. Slice, serve with green beans, and garnish with thyme sprigs.

STEAK, KIDNEY AND MUSHROOM PIE

A delicious dish with a wonderfully light and crisp pastry topping. This most famous of English recipes apparently dates from the 1850s.

INGREDIENTS

30ml/2 tbsp vegetable oil
115g/4oz bacon, chopped
1 onion, chopped
500g/1¼lb chuck steak, diced
25g/1oz/2 tbsp plain flour
115g/4oz lamb's kidneys
bouquet garni
400ml/14fl oz/1⅔ cups beef stock
115g/4oz button mushrooms
225g/8oz ready-made puff pastry
beaten egg, to glaze
salt and ground black pepper

SERVES 4

1 Preheat the oven to 160°C/325°F/Gas 3. Heat the oil in a heavy-based pan, add the bacon and onion and cook, stirring, until lightly browned.

2 Toss the steak in the flour, add to the pan in batches and cook, stirring, until browned. Toss the kidneys in the flour and add to the pan with the bouquet garni.

3 Transfer to a casserole, then pour in the stock, cover and cook for 2 hours. Stir in the mushrooms, season, then leave to cool.

4 Preheat the oven to 220°C/425°F/Gas 7. Roll out the pastry to 2cm/¾in larger than the top of a 1.2 litre/2 pint/5 cup pie dish. Cut off a strip and fit around the dampened rim of the dish. Brush with water.

5 Tip the meat mixture into the dish. Lay the pastry over the dish and press the edges together to seal. Knock up the edges with the back of a knife.

6 Make a small slit in the pastry, brush with beaten egg and bake for 20 minutes. Lower the oven to 180°C/350°F/Gas 4 and bake for a further 20 minutes.

LETTUCE AND HERB SALAD

Different types of lettuce are now available all year round, so try to use a mixture. Look out for pre-packed bags of mixed baby lettuce leaves.

INGREDIENTS
½ cucumber
mixed lettuce leaves
1 bunch watercress, about 115g/4oz
1 head of chicory, sliced
45ml/3 tbsp mixed chopped fresh herbs,
such as parsley, thyme, tarragon, chives
and chervil

FOR THE DRESSING
15ml/1 tbsp white wine vinegar
5ml/1 tsp prepared mustard
75ml/5 tbsp olive oil
salt and ground black pepper

SERVES 4

1 To make the dressing, spoon the vinegar and mustard into a small bowl or jug and mix together, then whisk in the oil and season to taste with salt and pepper.

2 Peel the cucumber, if liked, then halve it lengthways and scoop out the seeds. Thinly slice the flesh. Tear the lettuce leaves into bite-size pieces.

3 In a large salad bowl, mix together the cucumber, mixed lettuce leaves, watercress, chicory and chopped herbs.

4 Stir the dressing, then pour over the salad and toss lightly to coat the salad vegetables and leaves. Serve at once.

> ### COOK'S TIP
> Do not dress the salad until just before serving otherwise the lettuce leaves will wilt.

BUBBLE AND SQUEAK

T he name of this dish is derived from the bubbling of the vegetables as they are boiled and the way they squeak when they are fried.

INGREDIENTS
60ml/4 tbsp dripping, bacon fat or
vegetable oil
1 onion, finely chopped
450g/1lb potatoes, cooked and mashed
225g/8oz cooked cabbage or Brussels
sprouts, finely chopped
salt and ground black pepper

SERVES 4

1 Heat half of the dripping, fat or oil in a heavy frying pan. Add the onion and cook, stirring frequently, until softened.

2 Mix together the potatoes and cabbage or sprouts and season to taste with salt and plenty of pepper.

3 Add the vegetables to the pan, stir well, then press the vegetable mixture into a large, even cake.

4 Cook over a moderate heat for about 15 minutes, until the cake is browned underneath.

5 Hold a large plate over the pan, then invert the vegetable cake on to it. Add the remaining fat or oil to the pan, then, when it is hot, slip the cake back into the pan, browned side uppermost.

6 Cook the bubble and squeak over a moderate heat for a further 10 minutes, until the underside of the cake is golden brown, then serve hot, cut into wedges.

COOK'S TIP
If you don't have leftover cabbage or sprouts, use fresh vegetables instead. Chop roughly and cook in boiling salted water until just tender. Drain, chop again, then start the recipe.

BRAISED RED CABBAGE

Lightly spiced with a sharp, sweet flavour, braised red cabbage goes especially well with roast pork, duck and game dishes.

INGREDIENTS
1kg/2¼lb red cabbage
2 onions, chopped
2 cooking apples, peeled, cored and coarsely grated
5ml/1 tsp freshly grated nutmeg
1.5ml/¼ tsp ground cloves
1.5ml/¼ tsp ground cinnamon
15ml/1 tbsp dark brown sugar
45ml/3 tbsp red wine vinegar
25g/1oz/2 tbsp butter or margarine
salt and ground black pepper
fresh thyme sprigs, to garnish

SERVES 4–6

1 Cut off and discard the large white ribs from the outer leaves of the cabbages. Using a large serrated knife or the coarse holes on a grater, finely shred the cabbage.

2 Preheat the oven to 160°C/325°F/Gas 3. Layer the shredded cabbage in a large ovenproof dish with the onions, apples, nutmeg, cloves, cinnamon, sugar and seasoning. Pour over the wine vinegar. Cut the butter or margarine into cubes and scatter over the mixture.

3 Cover the dish and cook in the oven for about 1½ hours, stirring a couple of times, until the cabbage is very tender. Serve hot, garnished with thyme sprigs.

COOK'S TIP
This recipe can be cooked in advance. Bake the cabbage for 1½ hours, then leave to cool. To complete the cooking, bake in the oven at 160°C/325°F/Gas 3 for about 30 minutes, stirring the mixture occasionally.

LEMONY CARROTS

The carrots are cooked until just tender in a lemony stock which is then thickened to make a light, tangy sauce.

INGREDIENTS
600ml/1 pint/2½ cups water
450g/1lb carrots, thinly sliced
bouquet garni
15ml/1 tbsp lemon juice
pinch of freshly grated nutmeg
20g/¾oz/1½ tbsp butter
15ml/1 tbsp plain flour
salt and ground black pepper
fresh dill sprigs, to garnish

SERVES 4

1 Bring the water to the boil in a large pan, then add the carrots, bouquet garni, lemon juice, nutmeg and seasoning and simmer until the carrots are tender.

2 Remove the carrots from the pan with a slotted spoon, then cover and keep warm. Boil the cooking liquid hard until it is reduced to 300ml/½ pint/1¼ cups. Discard the bouquet garni.

3 Put 15g/½oz of the butter and the flour into a small bowl and mix with a fork.

4 Gradually whisk the mixture into the simmering liquid, whisking well after each addition. Simmer for about 3 minutes, until the sauce has thickened.

5 Return the carrots to the pan, heat them through in the sauce, then remove from the heat. Stir in the remaining butter and serve immediately, garnished with dill.

CAULIFLOWER
CHEESE

T his recipe may be adapted for vegetarians simply by omitting the bacon. It can be served as a main meal for lunch or supper or as a side-dish.

INGREDIENTS
1 cauliflower, broken into large florets
40g/1½oz/3 tbsp butter
1 small onion, chopped
2 streaky bacon rashers, chopped
45ml/3 tbsp plain flour
450ml/¾ pint/1⅞ cups milk
115g/4oz/1 cup grated mature
Cheddar cheese
pinch of English mustard powder
salt and ground black pepper

SERVES 4

1 Cook the cauliflower in boiling salted water until almost tender. Drain well and tip into a baking dish.

2 Meanwhile, melt the butter in a saucepan and gently cook the onion and bacon until the onion is soft, then spoon over the cauliflower.

3 Stir the flour into the butter in the pan and cook, stirring, for 1 minute. Remove the pan from the heat and slowly pour the milk into the pan, stirring all the time. Return the saucepan to the heat and bring to the boil, stirring constantly. Simmer for 4–5 minutes, stirring occasionally.

4 Preheat the grill. Remove the pan from the heat and stir in three-quarters of the grated cheese. Add the mustard and season to taste with salt and pepper.

5 Pour the sauce over the cauliflower and sprinkle the remaining cheese over the top. Heat the cauliflower cheese under the grill until the top is golden and bubbling.

PARSNIPS WITH ALMONDS

Parsnips have an affinity with most nuts, so you could substitute chopped walnuts or hazelnuts for the almonds, if you prefer.

INGREDIENTS
450g/1lb small parsnips
35g/1¼oz/scant 3 tbsp butter
25g/1oz/¼ cup flaked almonds
15ml/1 tbsp soft light brown sugar
pinch of ground mixed spice
15ml/1 tbsp lemon juice
salt and ground black pepper
fresh chervil sprigs, to garnish

SERVES 4

1 Cook the parsnips in boiling salted water until almost tender. Drain. When they are cool enough to handle, cut each in half across its width, then lengthways into quarters.

2 Melt the butter in a large frying pan. Add the parsnips and almonds and cook gently, stirring and turning the parsnips carefully until they are lightly flecked with brown and the almonds are golden brown. Do not let the almonds scorch.

3 Mix together the sugar and mixed spice, sprinkle over the parsnips and stir to mix, then trickle over the lemon juice. Season to taste with salt and pepper and heat for 1 minute. Serve garnished with chervil sprigs.

NEW POTATO AND CHIVE SALAD

T he secret of a good potato salad is to mix the potatoes with the dressing while they are still hot so that they absorb all the flavour.

INGREDIENTS
675g/1½lb new potatoes, unpeeled
4 spring onions
45ml/3 tbsp olive oil
15ml/1 tbsp white wine vinegar
5ml/1 tsp Dijon mustard
175ml/6fl oz/¾ cup mayonnaise
45ml/3 tbsp snipped fresh chives
salt and ground black pepper

SERVES 4–6

1 Cook the potatoes in boiling salted water until tender. Meanwhile, finely chop the white parts of the spring onions along with a little of the green part.

2 Whisk together the oil, vinegar and mustard. Drain the potatoes well, then immediately toss lightly with the dressing and spring onions and leave to cool.

3 Stir the mayonnaise and chives into the potatoes. Cover and chill well until required. Serve with grilled pork, lamb chops or roast chicken.

OLD ENGLISH TRIFLE

I f suitable fresh fruit is not in season, use canned varieties instead but make sure you drain them well before adding to the trifle.

INGREDIENTS
75g/3oz day-old sponge cake, broken into
bite-size pieces
8 ratafias, broken into halves
100ml/3½fl oz/⅓ cup medium sherry,
more if needed
30ml/2 tbsp brandy, more if needed
350g/12oz prepared fruit, such as
raspberries, strawberries or peaches
300ml/½ pint/1¼ cups double cream
40g/1½oz/⅓ cup toasted flaked almonds
and 2 or 3 strawberries, to decorate

FOR THE CUSTARD
4 egg yolks
25g/1oz caster sugar
450ml/¾ pint/1⅞ cups single or
whipping cream
few drops of vanilla essence

SERVES 6

1 Put the sponge cake and ratafias into a glass serving dish, then sprinkle over the sherry and brandy to taste and leave for about 1 hour until they have been absorbed. If the sponge cake or ratafias look dry, add more sherry and brandy.

2 To make the custard, whisk together the egg yolks and sugar in a large bowl. Pour the cream into a heavy saucepan and bring to the boil, then pour on to the egg yolk mixture, stirring constantly.

3 Return the mixture to the pan and heat very gently, stirring all the time with a wooden spoon, until the custard thickens enough to coat the back of the spoon; do not allow to boil. Add the vanilla essence. Leave the custard to cool, stirring occasionally.

4 Arrange the fruit in an even layer over the sponge cake in the serving dish, then strain the custard over the fruit and leave to set. Lightly whip the double cream, spread it over the custard, then chill the trifle well. Decorate with toasted flaked almonds and strawberries just before serving.

COOK'S TIP
To prevent custard from curdling, stir 5ml/1 tsp cornflour into the egg and caster sugar mixture, before adding the cream.

RHUBARB AND ORANGE FOOL

Perhaps this traditional pudding, which dates back to the sixteenth century, got its name because, like a trifle, it is a frivolous and light dessert.

INGREDIENTS

30ml/2 tbsp orange juice
5ml/1 tsp finely shredded orange rind
900g/2lb rhubarb, peeled and chopped
15ml/1 tbsp redcurrant jelly
45ml/3 tbsp caster sugar
150ml/¼ pint/⅔ cup double cream
150g/5oz prepared thick and creamy vanilla custard
sweet biscuits, to serve

SERVES 4

1 Place the orange juice and rind, the rhubarb, redcurrant jelly and sugar in a saucepan. Cover and simmer gently for about 8 minutes, stirring occasionally, until the rhubarb is just tender but not mushy.

2 Remove the pan from the heat, transfer the rhubarb to a bowl and leave to cool completely. Meanwhile, put the cream into a bowl and beat lightly.

3 Drain the cooled rhubarb to remove some of the liquid. Reserve about 30ml/ 2 tbsp of the rhubarb and a little orange rind for decoration. Purée the remaining rhubarb in a food processor or blender, or push it through a sieve. Stir the custard into the purée, then fold in the whipped cream (*right*) until smooth and evenly mixed.

4 Spoon the fool into individual bowls, cover and chill. Just before serving, top with the reserved fruit and rind. Serve with crisp, sweet biscuits.

BREAD AND BUTTER PUDDING

Vary the dried fruit in this pudding according to your preference. Use currants, sultanas, chopped dried apricots or a mixture of several sorts.

INGREDIENTS
75g/3oz/6 tbsp butter
6 slices white bread
50g/2oz/about ⅓ cup dried fruit
15ml/1 tbsp chopped mixed peel
50g/2oz/¼ cup soft light brown sugar
3 eggs, beaten
600ml/1 pint/2½ cups milk

SERVES 4–6

1 Butter a 1.2 litre/2 pint/5 cup baking dish. Butter the bread, then cut off the crusts and cut the slices into triangles, squares or fingers.

2 Arrange half of the bread in the baking dish. Scatter over the dried fruit, mixed peel and half of the sugar, then add the remaining bread.

COOK'S TIP
For a special occasion, use cream in place of some, or all, of the milk.

3 Beat together the eggs and milk, then pour into the dish. Sprinkle with the remaining sugar and leave to stand for at least 30 minutes. Meanwhile, preheat the oven to 160°C/325°F/Gas 3. Bake the pudding for 35–40 minutes, until set and crisp on top.

RASPBERRY MERINGUE GATEAU

A rich, hazelnut meringue filled with cream and raspberries makes a wonderful dessert served with a raspberry sauce.

INGREDIENTS
butter or margarine, for greasing
4 egg whites
225g/8oz/1 cup caster sugar
few drops of vanilla essence
5ml/1 tsp distilled malt vinegar
115g/4oz/1 cup roasted hazelnuts, ground
500g/1¼lb raspberries
45–60ml/3–4 tbsp icing sugar, sifted
15ml/1 tbsp orange liqueur
300ml/½ pint/1¼ cups double cream
icing sugar, for dusting
raspberries and fresh mint sprigs,
to decorate

SERVES 6

VARIATION
Fresh redcurrants make a good alternative to raspberries. Pick over the fruit, then pull each sprig gently through the prongs of a fork to release the redcurrants. Add them to the whipped cream with a little icing sugar, to taste.

1 Preheat the oven to 180°C/350°F/Gas 4. Grease two 20cm/8in sandwich tins and line the bases with rounds of greaseproof paper.

2 Whisk the egg whites in a large bowl until they hold stiff peaks, then gradually whisk in the caster sugar, 15ml/ 1 tbsp at a time, whisking well after each addition. Continue whisking the meringue mixture for a minute or two until very stiff, then fold in the vanilla essence, vinegar and ground hazelnuts.

3 Divide the meringue mixture between the prepared sandwich tins and spread it level. Bake for 50–60 minutes, until the meringue rounds are crisp. Remove the meringues from the tins and leave them to cool on a wire rack.

4 Meanwhile, make the raspberry sauce. Purée 225g/8oz of the raspberries with the icing sugar and orange liqueur in a blender or food processor, then press the purée through a fine nylon sieve to remove any pips. Chill the sauce until ready to serve.

5 Whip the cream until it forms soft peaks, then gently fold in the remaining raspberries. Sandwich the meringue rounds together with the raspberry cream.

6 Dust the top of the gâteau with icing sugar. Decorate with raspberries and mint sprigs and serve with the sauce.

COOK'S TIP
You can buy roasted chopped hazelnuts. Otherwise, toast whole hazelnuts and rub off the skins using a clean cloth.

SUMMER PUDDING

A quintessentially British way of serving fresh summer fruits which makes a welcome alternative to simply fruit and cream.

INGREDIENTS
about 8 thin slices day-old white bread,
crusts removed
750g/1¾lb summer fruits, such as
raspberries or a combination of
raspberries, redcurrants
and blackberries
about 30ml/2 tbsp sugar
30ml/2 tbsp water

SERVES 4

1 Cut a round from one slice of bread to fit in the base of a 1.2 litre/2 pint/5 cup pudding basin, then cut strips of bread about 5cm/2in wide to line the basin, overlapping the strips slightly so there are no gaps.

2 Place all the fruit in a large heavy saucepan, add the sugar and water and gently heat, shaking the pan occasionally, until the juices begin to run. Reserve about 45ml/ 3 tbsp fruit juice, then spoon the fruit and any remaining juice into the prepared basin, taking care not to dislodge any of the bread.

3 Cut the remaining bread to cover the fruit entirely. Put a saucer or small plate inside the top of the basin and place a heavy weight on top. Chill the pudding and the reserved fruit juice overnight.

4 Run a knife carefully around the inside of the basin rim, then invert the pudding on to a cold serving plate. Pour over the reserved juice and serve.

SHORTBREAD

Traditionally the shortbread dough is pressed into decorative wooden moulds, then turned out for baking. For really good shortbread, use only top-quality unsalted butter.

INGREDIENTS
115g/4oz/½ cup unsalted butter
50g/2oz/¼ cup caster sugar
115g/4oz/1 cup plain flour
50g/2oz/4 tbsp rice flour

MAKES 6–8 WEDGES

1 Preheat the oven to 160°C/325°F/Gas 3. Place a 15cm/6in plain flan ring on a baking sheet.

2 Beat together the butter and sugar until light and fluffy. Stir in both flours, then knead lightly until smooth.

3 Press the dough evenly into the flan ring, then lift the ring away. Crimp the edges of the dough with your thumb and finger.

4 Prick the surface of the shortbread with a fork and mark into six or eight wedges, then bake for 40 minutes, until pale biscuit coloured and just firm to the touch. Leave the shortbread to cool for a few minutes, then carefully transfer to a wire rack to cool completely. To serve, break the shortbread into wedges along the marked lines.

APPLE AND BLACKBERRY NUT CRUMBLE

This much-loved dish of Bramley apples and blackberries topped with a golden, sweet crumble is perhaps one of the simplest and most delicious of British hot desserts.

INGREDIENTS
butter, for greasing
900g/2lb/about 4 cooking apples, peeled, cored and sliced
115g/4oz/½ cup butter, cubed
115g/4oz/⅝ cup soft light brown sugar, firmly packed
15ml/1 tbsp water
175g/6oz/1¾ cups blackberries
75g/3oz/¾ cup wholemeal flour
75g/3oz/¾ cup plain flour
2.5ml/½ tsp ground cinnamon
45ml/3 tbsp chopped mixed nuts, toasted custard, cream or ice cream, to serve (optional)

SERVES 4

1 Preheat the oven to 180°C/350°F/Gas 4. Lightly butter a 1.2 litre/2 pint/5 cup ovenproof dish and set aside.

2 Place the apples in a large saucepan with 25g/1oz/2 tbsp of the butter, 30ml/2 tbsp of the sugar and the water. Cover and cook gently for about 10 minutes, until the apples are just tender but still holding their shape. Remove from the heat and gently stir in the blackberries. Spoon into the dish.

VARIATION
To make Plum Nut Crumble, omit the apples and blackberries and use 900g/2lb plums instead. Stone and halve the plums, put them in an ovenproof dish and sprinkle with 115g/4oz/⅝ cup soft light brown sugar. Make the nut crumble topping and bake as directed.

3 To make the crumble topping, sift the flours and cinnamon into a bowl (tip in any of the bran left in the sieve). Add the remaining butter and rub into the flour with your fingertips until the mixture resembles fine breadcrumbs (or you can use a food processor or blender, if you wish).

4 Stir in the remaining sugar and the nuts and mix well. Sprinkle the crumble topping evenly over the fruit. Bake for 35–40 minutes, until the topping is golden brown. Serve hot with custard, cream or ice cream, if wished.

LEMON MERINGUE PIE

A glorious dessert with a tart lemony filling, topped with a light-as-air sweet meringue and served on a sweet, almond flavoured pastry base.

INGREDIENTS
115g/4oz/1 cup plain flour
50g/2oz/4 tbsp butter, cubed
45ml/3 tbsp ground almonds
25g/1oz/2 tbsp sugar
1 egg yolk
30ml/2 tbsp cold water
flour, for rolling

FOR THE FILLING
juice of 3 lemons
finely grated rind of 2 lemons
45ml/3 tbsp cornflour
150ml/¼ pint/⅔ cup water
75g/3oz/6 tbsp sugar
2 egg yolks
15g/½oz/1 tbsp butter

FOR THE MERINGUE
2 egg whites
115g/4oz/½ cup caster sugar

MAKES A 19CM/7½IN PIE

1 To make the pastry, sift the flour into a bowl, add the butter and rub it in with your fingertips until the mixture resembles breadcrumbs (or use a food processor or blender). Stir in the ground almonds and sugar and add the egg yolk and cold water. Do not add too much water or the dough will be sticky and this makes the pastry tough. Mix with your hands until the pastry comes together.

2 Turn out the pastry on to a lightly floured surface and knead lightly, then wrap in clear film and chill for 30 minutes. Meanwhile, preheat the oven to 200°C/400°C/Gas 6 and put a baking sheet in the oven to heat up.

3 Roll out the pastry to a 20cm/8in round and use it to line a 19cm/7½in fluted loose-based flan tin. Prick the base. Line and fill with baking beans.

4 Place the tin on the baking sheet and bake for 12 minutes. Remove the paper and beans and bake for a further 5 minutes. Remove from the oven and cool. Reduce the oven temperature to 150°C/300°F/Gas 2.

5 To make the filling, put the lemon juice and rind into a measuring jug (you should have roughly 150ml/¼ pint/⅔ cup). Blend the cornflour with a little of the lemon juice, then gradually stir in the rest. Pour into a saucepan and add the water.

6 Bring slowly to the boil, stirring until smooth and thickened. Remove from the heat and beat in the sugar and egg yolks, then add the butter. Spoon the lemon mixture into the pastry case.

7 To make the meringue, whisk the egg whites until stiff, then gradually whisk in the sugar, 15ml/1 tbsp at a time, until thick and glossy. Pile the meringue on top of the lemon filling, spreading and swirling it with the back of a spoon. Bake for 30–35 minutes, or until the meringue is golden and crisp.

STICKY GINGERBREAD

Have napkins to hand when you serve this tea-time treat, as fingers will get gloriously sticky. Recipes for gingerbread date back to the Middle Ages.

INGREDIENTS

butter or margarine, for greasing
175g/6oz/1½ cups plain flour
10ml/2 tsp ground ginger
2.5ml/½ tsp ground cinnamon
2.5ml/½ tsp bicarbonate of soda
30ml/2 tbsp black treacle
30ml/2 tbsp golden syrup
75g/3oz/⅝ cup soft dark brown sugar
75g/3oz/6 tbsp butter
1 egg
15ml/1 tbsp milk
15ml/1 tbsp orange juice
2 pieces stem ginger, finely chopped
50g/2oz/½ cup sultanas
5 ready-to-eat dried apricots, chopped
45ml/3 tbsp icing sugar
10ml/2 tsp lemon juice

MAKES A 900G/2LB LOAF

1 Preheat the oven to 160°C/325°F/Gas 3. Grease and line the base of a 900g/2lb loaf tin with greaseproof paper. Sift the flour, spices and bicarbonate of soda into a bowl.

2 Place the treacle, syrup, sugar and butter in a pan and heat gently, until the butter has melted.

3 In a separate small bowl, beat together the egg, milk and orange juice.

4 Add the syrup mixture, egg mixture, chopped ginger, sultanas and apricots to the dry ingredients and stir well. Spoon into the prepared tin and level the top. Bake in the oven for about 50 minutes, or until the gingerbread is well risen and a skewer pierced through the centre comes out clean.

5 Remove the gingerbread from the oven, and leave to cool in the tin. Beat the icing sugar with the lemon juice in a bowl until smooth. Drizzle the icing over the top of the gingerbread, then leave to set.

SCONES

The versatile scone is not only a tea-time treat; when filled with fresh strawberries or raspberries instead of the jam, and spoonfuls of whipped cream, it becomes a delicious dessert.

INGREDIENTS
butter, for greasing
225g/8oz/2 cups plain flour
15ml/1 tbsp baking powder
50g/2oz/4 tbsp butter, cubed
1 egg, beaten
75ml/5 tbsp milk
flour, for rolling
beaten egg, to glaze
butter, jam and cream, to serve

MAKES 10–12

1 Preheat the oven to 220°C/425°F/Gas 7. Lightly butter a baking sheet. In a bowl, sift together the flour and baking powder, then rapidly rub in the butter using the tips of your fingers.

2 Make a well in the centre of the flour mixture, add the beaten egg and milk and mix to a soft dough using a round-bladed knife or a metal spatula.

3 Turn out the dough on to a floured surface and knead very lightly until smooth. Roll out to a 2cm/¾in thickness and cut into 10 or 12 rounds with a 5cm/2in plain or fluted cutter dipped in flour.

4 Transfer to the baking sheet, brush with egg, *(left)* then bake for about 8 minutes, until risen and golden. Cool slightly on a wire rack, then serve with butter, jam and cream.

SUMMER BERRY MEDLEY

Make the most of glorious seasonal fruits in this refreshing dessert. The sauce is also good swirled into Greek-style yogurt or strawberry-flavoured fromage frais.

INGREDIENTS
175g/6oz redcurrants
175g/6oz raspberries
50g/2oz/4 tbsp caster sugar
30–45ml/2–3 tbsp crème de framboise
450–675g/1–1½lb mixed soft summer fruits, such as strawberries, raspberries, blueberries, redcurrants and blackcurrants
vanilla ice cream, to serve (optional)

SERVES 4–6

1 Strip the redcurrants from their stalks with a fork and place them in a large bowl with the raspberries, sugar and crème de framboise. Cover and leave to macerate for 1–2 hours.

2 Transfer this fruit with its macerating juices to a large saucepan and cook gently for about 5 minutes, stirring occasionally, and taking care not to break up the fruit. Cook until the fruit is just tender when tested with a knife. Cool slightly.

3 Pour the hot fruit into a blender or food processor and process until smooth. Press the puréed fruit through a nylon sieve to remove any pips. Leave to cool, then cover and chill until ready to serve.

4 Divide the mixed soft fruit among individual glass serving dishes and pour the chilled sauce over the fruit. Serve the medley with scoops of vanilla ice cream if wished.

INDEX